REPTILES

GRAHAM MEADOWS & CLAIRE VIAL

Contents

About Reptiles

Reptiles make up one of the five main groups of **vertebrates**.

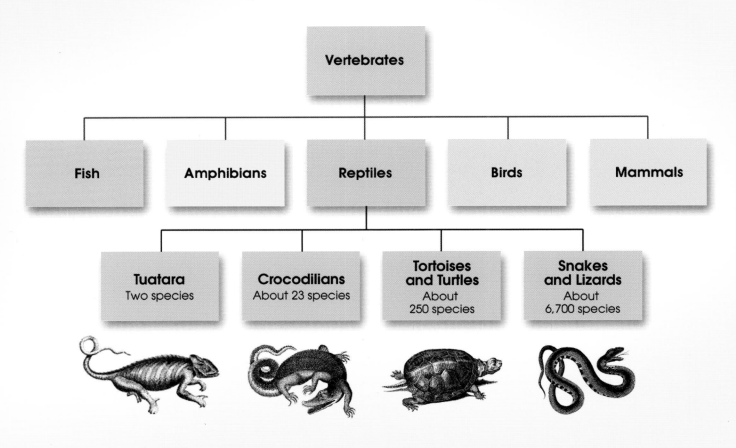

The study of reptiles and amphibians is called herpetology.

There are about 7,000 **species** of reptiles. Following are their chief characteristics:

Iguana

* All reptiles are cool-blooded. This means their body temperature is similar to that of their **environment**.

* Some reptiles, such as iguanas, have legs. Others do not.

* All reptiles have dry skin covered with scales or rough plates.

* Reptiles either lay eggs with shells, or the young hatch from eggs inside the mother just as the eggs are being laid.

MILLIONS OF YEARS AGO

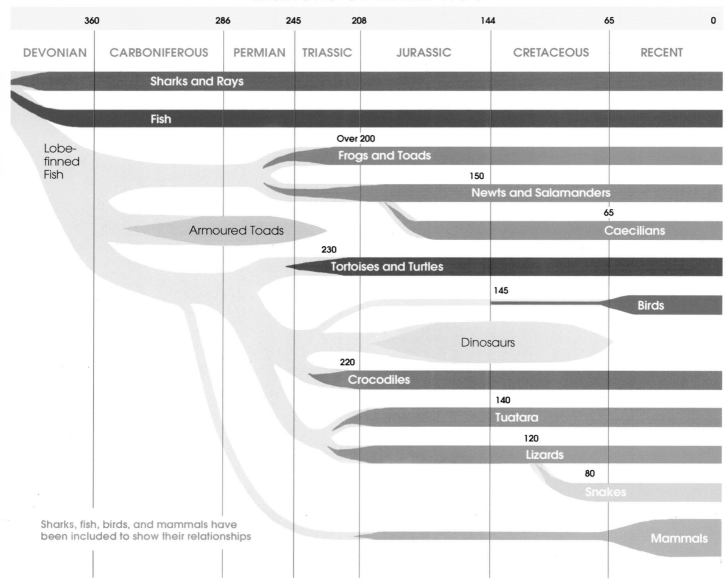

360	286	245	208	144	65	0

DEVONIAN | CARBONIFEROUS | PERMIAN | TRIASSIC | JURASSIC | CRETACEOUS | RECENT

Sharks and Rays

Fish

Lobe-finned Fish

Over 200
Frogs and Toads

150
Newts and Salamanders

65
Caecilians

Armoured Toads

230
Tortoises and Turtles

145
Birds

Dinosaurs

220
Crocodiles

140
Tuatara

120
Lizards

80
Snakes

Sharks, fish, birds, and mammals have been included to show their relationships

Mammals

4

How Reptiles Evolved

On the time line of **evolution,** scientists believe that reptiles evolved later than amphibians, but earlier than birds.

Judging by their study of **fossils,** many scientists think the evolution of reptiles began between 300 million and 350 million years ago. This was called the Carboniferous Period. They believe that reptiles evolved from amphibians.

Dinosaur

Reptiles were once the dominant animal group on earth. The dinosaurs lived on land. The plesiosaurs lived in the sea. And the pterodactyls flew in the air.

In addition to these giant reptiles, there were many other smaller reptiles. The giant reptiles became **extinct,** but many of the smaller reptiles **survived.** They were the **ancestors** of the reptile species we know today.

Types of Reptiles

Today's living reptiles are classified into four **orders**.

Order 1: Tuataras

There are two species of tuataras. They are the only living members of an ancient group of reptiles that lived more than 200 million years ago. Their **unique** features include a "third eye" on the top of their head, two rows of teeth in their upper jaw, and a rough crest along their back.

Tuatara

Leopard Tortoise   *Red-eared Turtle*

Order 2: Turtles and Tortoises

Turtles and tortoises are the only reptiles that have a bony shell that protects their bodies. They have a rough, horn-like beak instead of teeth. Most turtles live in water. Most tortoises live on land.

 Today, tuataras are found only on a few small islands off the coast of New Zealand.

Order 3: Crocodilians

Crocodilians are the largest and heaviest of the living reptiles. They are shaped like lizards and have a long snout. Their bodies are covered with very thick scales called plates. This order includes alligators, caimans, crocodiles, and gavials.

Order 4: Snakes and Lizards

Snakes and lizards make up the largest order of living reptiles. All lizards and snakes have scales, which are covered by skin. Most lizards have four legs, but snakes have none.

Alligator

Crocodile

Frill-necked Lizard

 Some lizards, such as worm lizards, slow-worms, and glass snakes, have no visible legs. They look like snakes.

Carpet Python ▶

Red-eared Turtle

 Reptiles can change the amount of blood that flows through the blood vessels near the surface of their skin.

Their Body Temperature

Since reptiles are cool-blooded animals, they need to use various methods to warm up and cool down.

Most reptiles warm up by sitting in the sun or lying on warm rocks. Some of them change color and are darker in the morning to absorb the sun's rays. Then they become lighter when it is hot so that they can reflect the sun's rays. If they get too hot, they move into the shade to cool down. This helps them keep their body at a temperature that is slightly higher than the temperature of their environment.

Lizard

Where Reptiles Live

Because pythons, water monitors, and other reptiles depend on warmth from their environment, they are not found in the Arctic, Greenland, Iceland, or Antarctica.

They are more commonly found in warmer **tropical** and subtropical regions than in cooler **temperate** regions. In warmer regions, reptiles live in a wide variety of **habitats.** These habitats include areas of freshwater and saltwater, swamps, grasslands, plains, and deserts.

◀ *Woma Python*

Water Monitor

In the mountains of the Himalayas and the Andes, some lizards can live as high up as 16,500 feet.

Fijian Banded Iguana

 Like other reptiles, Fijian banded iguanas have scales that help them retain water. This is especially important in dry, hot environments.

Their Skin and Scales

Reptiles are covered with a layer of scales. Their scales are really thick pieces of skin that are made of keratin, the same substance that makes up our fingernails. Because it is not elastic, reptiles must shed their skin from time to time as they grow.

Lizards shed their skin in pieces, but snakes shed their skin in one piece. Crocodile skin flakes off gradually and continually over time. Tortoises and turtles have hard, bony shells. As they grow, a new layer of keratin is added to each scale, which is called a plate. They only shed the skin on their heads, necks, legs, and tails.

Snake Skin ▶

Their Teeth and Tongues

Reptiles' teeth vary greatly in shape and size from one species to another. The teeth of lizards and snakes are very sharp and are attached directly to the jaw. They are not in sockets like the teeth of mammals. Crocodilian teeth are set in sockets and are not very sharp. Some snakes and lizards have poisonous teeth called fangs. Turtles and tortoises do not have teeth. Instead, they have a horn-like beak.

Reptiles use their tongues to "taste" scents in the air. Their tongues range in shape and size from long, forked, and very mobile to short, fleshy, and relatively **immobile**.

Crocodile Teeth ▶

◀ Monitor
Lizard Tongue

Carpet Python
Tongue ▼

Their Diet

Most reptiles eat other animals and swallow their food whole. When they are young, crocodilians feed on insects. But when they are fully developed, their **diet** includes fish, birds, mammals, and other reptiles. Most snakes feed on frogs, birds, birds' eggs, and small mammals. Most lizards eat insects and other **invertebrates**. Turtles eat a variety of foods, including water plants, insects, snails, fish, and frogs. Like other tortoises, the Galapagos tortoise depends on plants for the main part of its diet.

Galapagos Tortoise

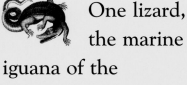 One lizard, the marine iguana of the Galapagos Islands, eats only seaweed.

◀ *Lizard*

Poisonous Reptiles

Gila Monsters

About one-fifth of all snake species, and two species of lizards, are **venomous**. Venomous snakes, such as rattlesnakes, have poison glands in their upper jaw that connect to their hollow fangs. When they strike, the poison is pumped through their fangs and into their victims.

The two poisonous species of lizards are the Gila monster, found in the southwestern United States, and the Mexican beaded lizard. These animals have poison glands in the lower jaw. The poison is not pumped into their victims, but instead flows along grooves on the surface of their lower teeth.

Most poisonous snakes use their venom to **paralyze** their **prey** before eating it whole.

Rattlesnake ▶

Reptile Eggs

Most reptiles lay their eggs on land. Most species lay eggs with a leathery shell. A few species lay eggs with a hard shell. Lizards bury their eggs under leaves or soil, or hide them in trees.

Tortoises, turtles, and some species of crocodiles dig holes and bury their eggs. In all these cases, the eggs **incubate** in the ground that has been warmed by the sun.

Turtle Laying Eggs ▸

Some reptile species, such as alligators and saltwater crocodiles, build mounds of vegetation in which they lay their eggs. The eggs incubate in the warmth of the rotting vegetation.

Crocodile on Mound

In cooler regions, some snakes and lizards incubate their eggs inside their bodies. The young hatch out as the eggs are being laid. This makes it look as if the female has given birth to live young.

 All young reptiles are able to feed themselves at birth.

Glossary

ancestors: Earlier related species
diet: The food that an animal or a person usually eats
environment: Setting; surroundings
evolution: Natural, gradual development
extinct: Species of animals and plants that are no longer alive
fossils: Preserved remains of an animal or a plant
habitats: The places where animals and plants live and grow
immobile: Unable to move
incubate: To keep warm
invertebrates: Animals that do not have a backbone
orders: Related families of organisms
paralyze: To make an animal unable to move
prey: Animals that are hunted and eaten by other animals
species: Types of animals that have something in common
survived: Stayed alive and thrived
temperate: Mild temperature; moderate climate
tropical: Areas that are very warm throughout the year
unique: Something that is different or special
venomous: Able to injure or kill prey with poison
vertebrates: Animals that have a spinal column and a well-developed brain

Index

Publisher: Raymond Yuen
Editor: Bob Rowland
Designer: Lois Stanfield, LightSource Images

Photo Credits: Graham Meadows Photography (cover photo–bottom right, and pages 5, 6, 7–right photo, 8–top photo, 9–bottom photo, 10, 14, 15, 17–bottom photo, and 19); New Zealand Picture Library (cover photo–bottom left, and pages 9–top photo, 12, 16, 21, and 22); Petr Necas (cover photo–top right); Steve Wilson\Nature Focus (cover photo–top left); Kerry Read (Page 3); Claire Vial Photography (pages 7–left photo, 8–bottom photo, 11, 13, and 17–top photo); Robin G. Bickford (Page 18); and ANT Photo Library (pages 20 and 23).

Published by:

Dominie Press, Inc.

1949 Kellogg Avenue
Carlsbad, California 92008 USA

Softcover Edition ISBN 0-7685-1635-8
Library Bound Edition ISBN 0-7685-1677-3

Printed in Singapore by PH Productions Pte Ltd
1 2 3 4 5 6 PH 04 03 02